I0765477

THE BASIS OF NLP TECHNIQUES

Tim Brunson, PhD

The International Hypnosis Research Institute, LLC

Copyright © 2020 The International Hypnosis
Research Institute, LLC

All rights reserved

No part of this book may be reproduced, or stored in a retrieval
system, or transmitted in any form or by any means, electronic,
mechanical, photocopying, recording, or otherwise, without
express written permission of the publisher.

CONTENTS

INTRODUCTION

Although I have been officially certified as a NLP trainer and completed my trainers-training course with people who assisted Richard Bandler early on in their career, I am going to take somewhat of a different approach to how I present NLP techniques. Like my other books on topics such as Elman and Erickson methodologies, I want you to first understand the underlying concepts rather than have you learn and practice a bunch of techniques without understanding what you are doing.

NLP AND HYPNOSIS

I want to start by explaining the relationship between NLP and hypnosis. As the initial development of the field was heavily influenced by Dr. Erickson's work, obviously reviewing his approach would be in order.

Erickson looked at therapy as a process that respected the natural healing tendency of the subject. Predominately, he felt that a person who was experiencing any dysfunctionality was faced with the need to split the relationship between the state and behavior. Of course, you are most likely already seeing the relationship between Erickson's philosophy and the NLP Communication Model. What he would attempt to do is to split the linkage between perception, filters, state, and behavior, and to create a new one. He wanted the new linkage to represent a more functional alternative. His techniques were designed to accomplish this splitting and re-linking. He found that a trance state assisted with the splitting and linking process.

His approach was often much more permissive than what many lay people would expect. Rather than the more direct or authoritarian approaches used by stage hypnotists and many of the hypnotists of his day, he preferred to suggest a response rather than telling a subject what they would experience. To do this he frequently would use confusing linguistic techniques that tended to disturb a person's state, thereby creating the splitting that I just referred to. Then he would rely on the subject's natural ability to return to a more comfortable state. This he hoped would lead them to a more acceptable condition.

When Grinder and Bandler studied Erickson, they applied his methods albeit in a more algorithmic way. Again, the goal is to use NLP interventions in a way that changes a person's filters, internal representations, emotional states, and behaviors.

Let's look at this for a moment from the Advanced Neuro-Noetic Hypnosis standpoint. In ANNH I define hypnosis as a process that reduces pattern resistance, which is pretty much the same as inertia or resistance to change and empowers more efficient selective thinking. The splitting attribute of Ericksonian hypnosis and many NLP techniques accomplishes the pattern resistance component of my definition of hypnosis. The naturalistic attainment of a solution is very similar to what

I am referring to as more efficient selective thinking.

I want to take this one step further. One of the most important ANNH concepts is Pattern Theory, which states that everything around us and in us is organized in patterns of components that have structure, encoding, and can be activated or recalled. This applies to the components of the NLP Communication Model. Additionally, I point out that patterns will naturally resist change but experience a transformative entrainment when there is an antithetical change in its environment. Therefore, if a significant change is perceived, the filters may alter, the internal representation may change, the emotional and feeling state will become modified, and a different behavior will result.

When any pattern component changes radically enough – a condition that I refer to as being antithetical – the other components will adjust so that a sense of harmony will again be established. For instance, purposefully change behavior and state, internal representation, and filters will change. Change a filter and internal representation, emotional state, and behavior will change. And so on. Therefore, getting a person to walk or stand in a different manner or position, or having them intentionally change an internal representation – as is done in reframing or parts integration techniques – will precipitate a pattern change. As you read the next few books in this series, please keep this in mind.

In ANNH terminology what we are doing with most if not all NLP techniques is merely changing the encoding of a component of the NLP Communication Model – or pattern as I prefer to call it – and expecting a re-harmonization. Like Erickson, we are relying on the natural tendency for the subject to find a new, more harmonious alternative. What we are looking for is a new AH-HA moment.

MANIPULATING SPACE/TIME PERCEPTIONS

Students, who have read my other ANNH-oriented books, know that when I talk about changing a component's encoding, I am referring to an alteration of the attributes related to that component. Mathematically this is like changing the coefficient assigned to a variable. For instance, 1x becomes 3x. For the NLP Communication Model components, it is surprisingly simple. Just look how the concept of space and time affects filters and internal representations.

A person's filters help them judge both where and when they are in both space and time. At this point you know either generally or exactly the time of day and where your body is in relationship to the surrounding people and objects. This gives you a firm sense of your personal reality.

Also, if you consider the concept of timelines, if you think about it, when you refer to your past you may point to your left or right or behind you. You may feel that your future is in just the opposite direction. The Time-Line Therapy concept that was developed and trademarked by Tad James, PhD, is based largely on recognizing the shape and orientation of your personal timeline and when and how to alter it. Again, I refer to this as a re-encoding of a filter and/or internal representation.

Many of the more traditional NLP interventions seek to alter the encoding of the internal representations of space and time. There is a post-Grinder and Bandler NLP technique called the Disney Strategy. It is an adaptation of a management technique used by the creative genius. It recognizes that decision makers play three distinct roles, which are: The Dreamer, The Realist, and The Critic.

The Dreamer forms new ideas and goals, The Realist transforms ideas into concrete expressions, and The Critic acts as a stimulus for refinement of the ideas. In the NLP technique the subject is asked to associate into each of these roles. As they do, they are asked to physically stand in a different location. This provides a spatial anchor for each role association. Typically, the practitioner will also place a different color large card at each location. This provides an additional encoding quality to each position.

As the subject is moved from one position to the other their internal representation changes. When they are in The Dreamer position, they are expected to fully associate into that role. The Practitioner looks for physiological signs that the subject has achieved a peak emotional state. The goal is to allow the series of associations to create a synthesis of each role and hopefully create a more productive solution or course of action. Again, it is the intention that the subject naturally derive an intuitive resolution. You should note that such a revelation is much more powerful, as they have complete ownership of it.

There are several other examples of NLP interventions that use space as a way of re-encoding an internal representation or filter. One very popular technique is called the VK Dissociation Phobia "Cure" in which the subject is encouraged to see themselves sitting in a theater watching a screen where the initiating event is being played. This is an example of a double dissociation as they are suggested to see their dissociated selves. By the way, if you are tempted to try this immediately, I suggest that you do not until you have received further instruction. When teaching this technique, I explain the importance of safety as you do not wish the intervention to create a severe revivication, which in turn could do severe psychological damage to the subject.

Altering the perception of time is another prime example of changing the encoding of filters and internal representations. Going back to the Disney Strategy for a moment, I wish to point out that each one of the roles has a specific time orientation. The Dreamer is future oriented, The Realist is oriented in the present, and The Critic tends to be oriented both in the past and the future simultaneously. When I teach this intervention, I also get my students to notice how the subject's physiology is altered as they associate into each position.

Although I have focused on space and time somewhat separately until now, as just implied regarding the Disney Strategy, they may be blended. One example of this is having the subject to regress or progress through time while "walking the timeline." When this is done, the Practitioner and subject establish a line on the floor that represents their subject's past, present, and future. The Practitioner gently moves the subject back along their timeline to specific positions that may represent significant events – to include initiating events – in their lives.

Once they are there, the subject may be asked questions about how they represent the memory in their mind. Again, safety needs to be a factor during this exercise. Once they are at a specific space and time position, the Practitioner may suggest a change in how they represent this event in terms of submodalities. (I'll discuss submodalities in just a few moments.) They may also find it necessary to ask the subject to step off the timeline and imagine that they are viewing themselves at a distance. This is helpful when the Practitioner is seeking to disempower a negative association.

Finding or addressing negative events is not the only advantage of this timeline exercise. A Practitioner may also use this to go back into a person's past and help them find events or other resources that represent their strength or symbolize safety and security. These resources can then be taken back to the difficult events to help them diffuse painful memories. They can also be taken forward into their future.

Before I leave space and time concepts, I want to mention why they are important from the ANNH perspective. Our brain is designed to protect us – or at least to protect the known and accepted patterns with which we are familiar. Anything that is perceived to be within our present space and time, which is also referred to as peripersonal, will garner a stronger neurological reaction. So, deciding how an event or concept is to be represented in space and time will significantly change how the mind accepts it. This is a very critical concept when it comes to enhancing performance, resolving mental pathologies, and achieving self-actualization. The topic is so significant that I have written a separate book entitled *Space/Time-Based Interventions*.

SUBMODALITIES

Another category of encoding change involves what NLP Practitioners call submodalities. Here we are referring to modalities as the same perceptual preferences discussed in the *Mastering the NLP Communication Model* book. Again, these are Visual, Auditory, Kinesthetic, Olfactory, and Gustatory – or seeing, hearing, feeling, smelling, and tasting. When we change the intensity, we say that we are changing the submodalities. Here are some examples.

Have your subject think of a memory that was pleasant or enjoyable. Chances are they will see it as being through their eyes – meaning that it is an associated memory – in color, near, and vivid. However, changing the same memory so that it is perceived as dissociated – meaning that they are seeing themselves at a distance, in black and white, and fuzzy will significantly change their state.

When applied to other modalities, submodalities work much the same. The memory of a sound can be louder and clearer or softer and harder to hear. Taste can be sweet, bland, or repulsive. And a smell can be pleasant or very offensive.

EMPOWERMENT AND DISEMPOWERMENT

A Practitioner can then suggest changes to a submodality to alter the subject's internal representation. As an example, when a visual memory is associated, clear, in color, and vivid, the representation will precipitate a very distinct state. If it is a positive memory, the state will be enjoyable. However, should the memory be an unpleasant one – such as a recall of an initiating event for a phobia – the intensity of the emotion may create a significant revivication – which may be dangerous at times. The solution at this point would be to suggest that the subject intentionally change the submodalities of the representation so that their state would positively change.

In summary, by changing the submodalities of the

memory you can change their state. If it is a desired state, such as happiness and excitement, alter the submodalities so that they are emotionally impactful. This is synonymous with empowerment. If you wish to negate or de-program the memory, change the submodalities accordingly. This means suggest a dissociation and turn down the submodalties.

Submodality changes can also be blended with space/time considerations. For instance, I would ask a subject to see a positive memory on an imaginary TV monitor that is floating somewhere in the room. I make sure that their submodalities include associations that have vivid, clear, and favorable qualities.

After I break their state by asking them neutral questions that are totally unrelated to the intervention, I ask them to think of a negative memory and ask them where that monitor is floating. At that point I inquire as to the modalities related to that representation. They typically will inform me that the monitor is at a different location. However, the submodalities are again associated, vivid, and clear. I ask them to intentionally change their submodalities so that they are dissociated and fuzzy. I may even ask them to imagine that the monitor is starting to move away rapidly and getting smaller and smaller until it disappears.

Next, I will ask them to look at the position where

their positive monitor was previously. I will ask them to recall the negative memory and relate to me their internal state. At that point they almost always tell me that they have difficulty experiencing the previously painful negative memory. This is usually a shocking experience for the subject as they can no longer experience the pain of that memory.

DEMONSTRATION

You may wish to find a comfortable place where you can sit undisturbed for several moments. If you like, you may also find your experience will deepen should you close your eyes. I want you to consider this situation.

Today you are a golfer. You are standing on the putting green with your ball on the grass about eleven feet from the hole. Your goal is to strike the ball with your putter with enough power and authority to move it all the way to the hole and gently enough not to overshoot it.

Here goes:

"For a moment I would like you to close your eyes and become aware of the sensations of your body. You may even want to briefly scan your body from head to toe. As you do, begin allowing your body to relax comfortably. Become increasingly aware of the temperature of your skin. Perhaps you may wish to imagine that a layer of energy resides just a half inch or two beyond the physical limits of your skin.

As you increasingly become comfortable with the awareness of this energy around your body, begin imagining the feeling of the grip of your putter in your two hands. Enjoy the feeling. Imagine your energy transmitting down the shaft of the putter all the way down to the head. Imagine the putter as being an extension of your body. Your putter begins to feel the coolness of the air passing by it. Even as it touches your ball, you feel the sensation just as if you are touching it with your fingers. Hard. You sense its potential. Feeling the whiteness and the dimples of the ball.

Now let your energy expand to the space around you. Let it slowly expand. Perhaps a foot, then five, eight, ten, and even eleven. You sense the hole. The shape. Its width and depth. You begin to imagine your ball traveling with just the right amount of force. Rolling perfectly upon the ground. Moving easily toward the hole. Naturally following the path. Rolling easily to the hole. Falling in. You sense it falling almost like in slow motion. Falling. You hear it dropping in your mind. Letting it happen. Feeling the satisfaction of a perfect putt. You enjoy the sensation. Allowing it to happen. Now as your mind feels comfortable and relaxed. You may wish to allow yourself to begin returning. When ready you may open your eyes."

ABOUT THE AUTHOR

This series is by Tim Brunson, who holds both Doctor of Clinical Hypnotherapy and Doctor of Philosophy Clinical Hypnotherapy degrees, has practiced hypnotherapy for 29 years with clients and patients referred to him by medical and mental health practitioners, has trained clinicians internationally, and has almost 3,000 hours of training much of which was medical and mental health related. Many of his courses are already available through Amazon in either short-read or longer books.

RESOURCES

General:

The International Hypnosis Research Institute

IHRI membership

Advanced-Neuro-Noetic-Hypnosis

Courses

Books, E-Books, And Audiobooks:

Sets

Elman Hypnotherapy: Beyond the Basics

Improving Your Performance Genius

Enhancing Performance: Unleashing Your True Potential (Bundled)

Innovations in Mind/Body Therapies

The Mind/Body Connection

The New Biology

The Neurology of Mind/Body Health

Transformation Revisited

The Immune System Primer

Using Imagery to Heal

A Quick Pain Management Primer

Healing the Body Basics

The Mind, Surgery, and Recovery

Calming Your Gut

Innovations in Mind/Body Therapies (Bundled)

The Neurology of Suggestion Series

The Neurology of Suggestion

Advanced Hypnotherapy Protocols and Applications

The Neurology of Suggestion Series (Bundled)

The Neurology of Suggestion Basics

Change: A New Paradigm for Transformation

Brain Potential: Enhancing and Inhibiting for Peak Performance

Reshaping: Changing your Brain and Body

Individual Books

Advanced Hypnotherapy Script Writing Techniques

Clinical Hypnotherapy Fundamentals

Healing the Body

Healing the Mind

New Directions in Hypnotherapy

Rapid Change: The Secrets of Lasting Personal and Group Transformation

Space/Time-based Interventions: Simple techniques that enhance hypnotherapy.

www.ingramcontent.com/pod-product-compliance
Lightning Source LLC
Chambersburg PA
CBHW061550250726

48657CB00006B/2400